THE TRiPLETS

My First Picture
Dictionary

German-English

Illustrations: From the original drawings of Roser Capdevila
Text: Isabel Carril

CONTENTS

● Family and friends   4

    Our family   6
    Our friends   8
    Family and friends   10
● The house   12

    Our dining-living room   14
    Our bedroom   16
    Our kitchen   18
    Our bathroom   20
    The house   22
● The school   24

    Our classroom   26
    Our playground   28
    The school   30
● The city   32

    Our street   34
    The trip   36
    What would you like to do when you grow up?   38
    Sports   40
    The city   42
● Animals and plants   44

    Let's go to the farm   46
    Let's go to the zoo   48
    Let's go to the aquarium   50
    Animals and plants   52
● Index   54

My First Picture
Dictionary

German-English

This picture dictionary introduces children to the marvellous world of words with colourful illustrations and simple translations.

Words are the key to a child's understanding of the world, and a sound acquisition of first words lays the foundations of successful language learning.

Learning is kept fun as children are guided through the pages of this picture dictionary by recurrent characters – young triplets. Children acquire new vocabulary and use their skills of observation, while they get to know the triplets' family, friends and school.

Parents can also suggest games to play, from searching for individual objects as well as the triplets in the larger illustrations, to answering the questions asked in the first and final pages of each chapter.

The games on the opening spread of each chapter are designed to introduce children to the chapter's theme. For example, in Family and friends, readers search the illustration for characters with particular attributes: tall, short, blond...

In the last spread of each chapter, words are introduced to explain how they are used to form sentences. For example, the final spread of Family and friends features words related to the expression "Who is it?" and "What are they doing?". Children can respond to these questions out loud, search for answers in the big illustrations throughout the chapter, and even use them to construct their own sentences.

Children will really enjoy expanding their vocabulary with this picture dictionary – and parents and teachers can join them in exploring the fascinating world of words.

Die familie und die Freunde
Family and friends

Finde jemanden, der … ist
Find someone who is…

GROSS
TALL

KLEIN
SHORT

DICK
STOUT

DÜNN
THIN

Finde jemanden, der … hat
Find someone who has…

BLONDES HAAR
BLOND HAIR

DUNKLES HAAR
DARK HAIR

LANGES HAAR
LONG HAIR

KURZES HAAR
SHORT HAIR

GLATTES HAAR
STRAIGHT HAIR

LOCKIGES HAAR
CURLY HAIR

Unsere Familie
Our family

GROSSVATER
GRANDFATHER

GROSSMUTTER
GRANDMOTHER

VATER
FATHER

MUTTER
MOTHER

SOHN
SON

TOCHTER
DAUGHTER

BRÜDER
BROTHERS

SCHWESTER
SISTER

ENKEL
GRANDSON

ENKELIN
GRANDDAUGHTER

COUSIN
COUSIN

COUSINE
COUSIN

BABY
BABY

ZWILLINGE
TWINS

XYLOPHON
XYLOPHONE

TAMBURIN
TAMBOURINE

KLAVIER
PIANO

GEIGE
VIOLIN

TROMPETE
TRUMPET

GUITARRE
GUITAR

TROMMEL
DRUM

GLÜHBIRN
BULB

GELANGWEILT
BORED

KOMISCH
FUNNY

TRAURIG
SAD

GLÜCKLICH
HAPPY

MÜDE
TIRED

KONFETTI
CONFETTI

Unsere Freunde
Our friends

BALLPOOL
BALL POOL

KEGEL
SKITTLES

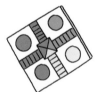

LUDO
LUDO

PUZZLE
JIGSAW
PUZZLE

HANDPUPPE
PUPPET

KERZEN
CANDLES

ROLLER
SCOOTER

BRÖTCHEN
BUNS

BAUSTEINE
BUILDING BLOCKS

KARTEN
CARDS

SCHLOSS
CASTLE

SKATEBOARD
SKATEBOARD

COMPUTERSPIEL
COMPUTER GAME

PUPPEN
DOLLS

LIMONADE
SOFT DRINKS

ROBOTER
ROBOT

BALLON
BALLOON

DREIRAD
TRICYCLE

FREUNDE
FRIENDS

VERKLEIDUNG
FANCY DRESS

BARFUSS
BAREFOOT

SCHUHE TRAGEND
WEARING SHOES

IRATENSCHIFF
PIRATE SHIP

FLAGGE
FLAG

KUCHEN
CAKE

SPIELKÜCHE
TOY KITCHEN

SAUBER
CLEAN

SCHMUTZIG
DIRTY

Die Familie und die Freunde
Family and friends

ONKEL
UNCLE

TANTE
AUNT

NEFFE
NEPHEW

NICHTE
NIECE

KÜSSEN
TO KISS

LESEN
TO READ

REDEN
TO TALK

SCHREIEN
TO SHOUT

UMARMEN
TO HUG

Wer ist das?
Who is it?

Was machen sie?
What do they do?

STREICHELN
TO CARESS

APPLAUDIEREN
TO APPLAUD

TANZEN
TO DANCE

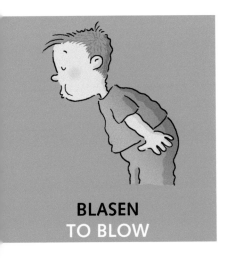

BLASEN
TO BLOW

FALLEN
TO FALL

BINDEN
TO TIE

GÄHNEN
TO YAWN

SINGEN
TO SING

ZUHÖREN
TO LISTEN

Das Haus
The house

Wo befindet sich jedes Bild?
Where is each picture?

Befindet es sich rechts oder links von den Drillingen?
Is it to the right or to the left of the triplets?

FENSTER

WINDOW

JALOUSIE

BLIND

BALKON

BALCONY

SCHORNSTEIN

CHIMNEY

NACHBAR

NEIGHBOUR

TÜR

DOOR

ROHR

PIPE

ZAUN

FENCE

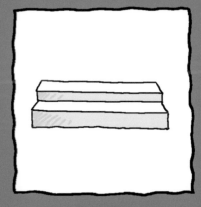

STUFEN

STEPS

Unser Wohnzimmer
Our dining-living room

VORHANG
CURTAIN

BUCH
BOOK

LAMPE
LAMP

TISCHDECKE
TABLECLOTH

SERVIETTE
NAPKIN

GLAS
GLASS

REGAL
BOOKSHELF

VASE
VASE

SESSEL
ARMCHAIR

DVD
DVD

GARDINE
NET CURTAIN

BILD
PICTURE

FERNSEHER
TELEVISION

SOFA
SOFA

STECKER
PLUG

KRUG
JUG

TEPPICH
RUG

HI-FI ANLAGE
HI-FI

TELLER
PLATE

TELEFON
TELEPHONE

BODEN
FLOOR

MESSER
KNIFE

GABEL
FORK

FLASCHE
BOTTLE

UHR
CLOCK

LAUTSPRECHER
SPEAKER

SALZFÄSSCHEN
SALTCELLAR

DECKE
CEILING

Unser Schlafzimmer
Our bedroom

ROCK
SKIRT

SCHLÜPFER
KNICKERS

BEDDECKE
EIDERDOWN

SCHUBLADE
DRAWER

JACKE
JACKET

MORGENMANTEL
DRESSING GOWN

SCHLAFANZUG
PYJAMAS

NACHTHEMD
NIGHTDRESS

STOCKBETTEN
BUNK BEDS

PULLOVER
JUMPER

KLEID
DRESS

SCHRANK
WARDROBE

SCHREIBTISCH
DESK

UNTERHOSEN
UNDERPANTS

KINDERBETT
COT

SOCKEN
SOCKS

DECKE
BLANKET

REISSVERSCHLUSS
ZIP

KNOPF
BUTTON

HOSE
TROUSERS

T-SHIRT
T-SHIRT

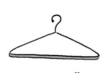

KLEIDERBÜGEL
HANGER

STIEFEL
BOOTS

JOGGINGSCHUHE
TRAINERS

HAUSSCHUHE
SLIPPERS

SCHUHE
SHOES

LEINTUCH
SHEET

KOPFKISSEN
PILLOW

Unsere Küche
Our kitchen

HERD
COOKER

TABLETT
TRAY

PFANNE
FRYING PAN

KÜHLSCHRANK
FRIDGE

FLEISCH
MEAT

FISCH
FISH

FRÜCHTE
FRUIT

SIEB
COLANDER

ZUCKERDOSE
SUGAR BOWL

JOGURT
YOGURT

OFEN
OVEN

MIKROWELLE
MICROWAVE

ABFALLEIMER
RUBBISH BIN

CAFETIERE PERCOLATOR
COFFEE POT

TOPF
POT

BESEN
BRUSH

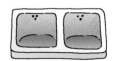

KÜCHENSPÜLE
SINK

WASSERHAHN
TAP

GESCHIRR-SPÜLMASCHINE
DISHWASHER

GEFRIERTRUHE
FREEZER

WASCHMASCHINE
WASHING
MACHINE

GEMÜSE
VEGETABLES

MILCH
MILK

FRÜHSTÜCKSFLOCKEN
CEREAL

SCHOKOLADE
CHOCOLATE

BROT
BREAD

KEKS
BISCUIT

SAFT
JUICE

Unser Badezimmer
Our bathroom

ARM
ARM

ELLBOGEN
ELBOW

HAND
HAND

FINGER
FINGER

KNIE
KNEE

SCHULTER
SHOULDER

BRUST
BREAST

RÜCKEN
BACK

BEIN
LEG

FUSS
FOOT

KNÖCHEL
ANKLE

HINTERN
BOTTOM

STIRN
FOREHEAD

AUGE
EYE

KLOPAPIER
TOILET PAPER

ZAHNPASTA
TOOTHPASTE

WASCHBECKEN
WASHBASIN

TOILETTE
TOILET

SCHWAMM
SPONGE

SEIFE
SOAP

HANDTUCHHALTER
TOWEL RACK

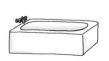

BAD
BATH

NASE
NOSE

OHR
EAR

MUND
MOUTH

ZÄHNE
TEETH

ZUNGE
TONGUE

HALS
NECK

Das Haus
The house

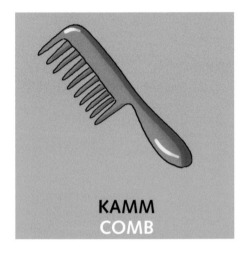

KAMM
COMB

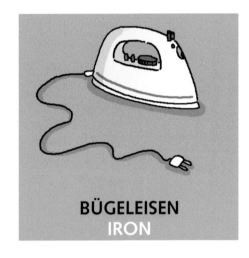

BÜGELEISEN
IRON

DUSCHE
SHOWER

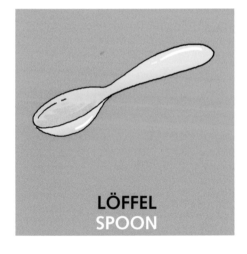

LÖFFEL
SPOON

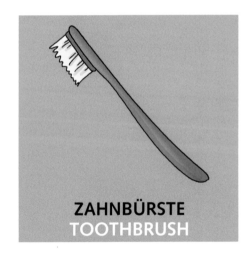

ZAHNBÜRSTE
TOOTHBRUSH

SPIEGEL
MIRROR

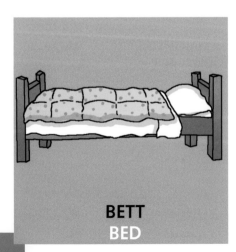

BETT
BED

GLAS
GLASS

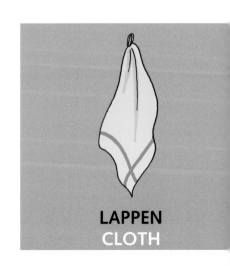

LAPPEN
CLOTH

Was ist es?
What is it?

Wofür benutzt man es?
What is it used for?

KÄMMEN
TO COMB

BÜGELN
TO IRON

DUSCHEN
TO TAKE A SHOWER

ESSEN
TO EAT

ZÄHNE PUTZEN
TO BRUSH YOUR TEETH

SICH ANSCHAUEN
TO LOOK AT YOURSELF

SCHLAFEN
TO SLEEP

TRINKEN
TO DRINK

PUTZEN
TO CLEAN

Die Schule
The school

Ich sehe, ich sehe… etwas… . Welche Farbe hat es? Gelb! Was ist es? Ein Kücken!

I spy, I spy… Something… What colour is it? Yellow! What is it? A chick!

GELB
YELLOW

BLAU
BLUE

ROT
RED

GRÜN
GREEN

ORANGE
ORANGE

BRAUN
BROWN

LILA
PURPLE

WEISS
WHITE

SCHWARZ
BLACK

Unser Klassenzimmer
Our classroom

COMPUTER
COMPUTER

WISCHER
DUSTER

RADIERGUMMI
ERASER

GRABSTICHEL
BURIN

KREIDE
CHALK

MÄPPCHEN
PENCIL CASE

KÄFIG
CAGE

BLATT PAPIER
SHEET OF PAPER

KLEBESTIFT
GLUE STICK

LÄTZCHEN
BIB

STIFT
PEN

STUHL
CHAIR

WACHSSTIFTE
WAX CRAYONS

HAMSTER
HAMSTER

NOTIZBUCH
NOTEBOOK

WANDGEMÄLDE
MURAL

TISCH
TABLE

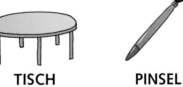

PINSEL
PAINTBRUSH

SPITZER
PENCIL
SHARPENER

FARBEN
PAINTS

AQUARIUM
FISHTANK

TAFEL
BLACKBOARD

BLEISTIFT
PENCIL

FALTER
FOLDER

KNET
MODELLING PASTE

LINEAL
RULER

SCHERE
SCISSORS

REGAL
SHELF

Unser Spielplatz
Our playground

BALL
BALL

BELEGTES BROT
SANDWICH

TRINKBRUNNEN
FOUNTAIN

BANK
BENCH

SCHAUKELN
SWINGS

TOR
GOALPOST

RUTSCHE
SLIDE

KREISEL
SPINNING TOP

PFEIFE
WHISTLE

MURMELN
MARBLES

WASSER
WATER

BAUM
TREE

BILDKARTEN
PICTURE CARDS

JOJO
YO-YO

PAPIERFLUGZEUG
PAPER PLANE

RUCKSACK
BACKPACK

RECHEN
RAKE

BLÄTTER
LEAVES

SAND
SAND

HÜPFSEIL
SKIPPING ROPE

HANDSCHUHE
GLOVES

SCHLEIFE
BOW

SCHAUFEL
SHOVEL

KLEINER VOGEL
LITTLE BIRD

BLUMENTOPF
FLOWERPOT

EIMER
BUCKET

REIFEN
HOOPS

BRILLE
GLASSES

Die Schule
The school

LEHRER
TEACHER

SCHIEDSRICHTER
REFEREE

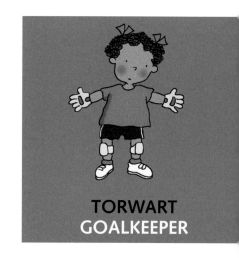

TORWART
GOALKEEPER

SPRINGEN
TO JUMP

WEINEN
TO CRY

LACHEN
TO LAUGH

AUFPRALLEN LASSEN
TO BOUNCE

HOCHSTEIGEN
TO GO UP

HERUNTERRUTSCHEN
TO GO DOWN

Was tun sie?
What do they do?

Wie geht es ihnen?
How are they?

Wo ist es?
Where is it?

WERFEN
TO THROW

RENNEN
TO RUN

STEHEN
STANDING

SITZEN
SITTING

KNIEN
ON YOUR KNEES

OBEN
UP

UNTEN
DOWN

INNEN
INSIDE

AUSSEN
OUTSIDE

Die Stadt
The city

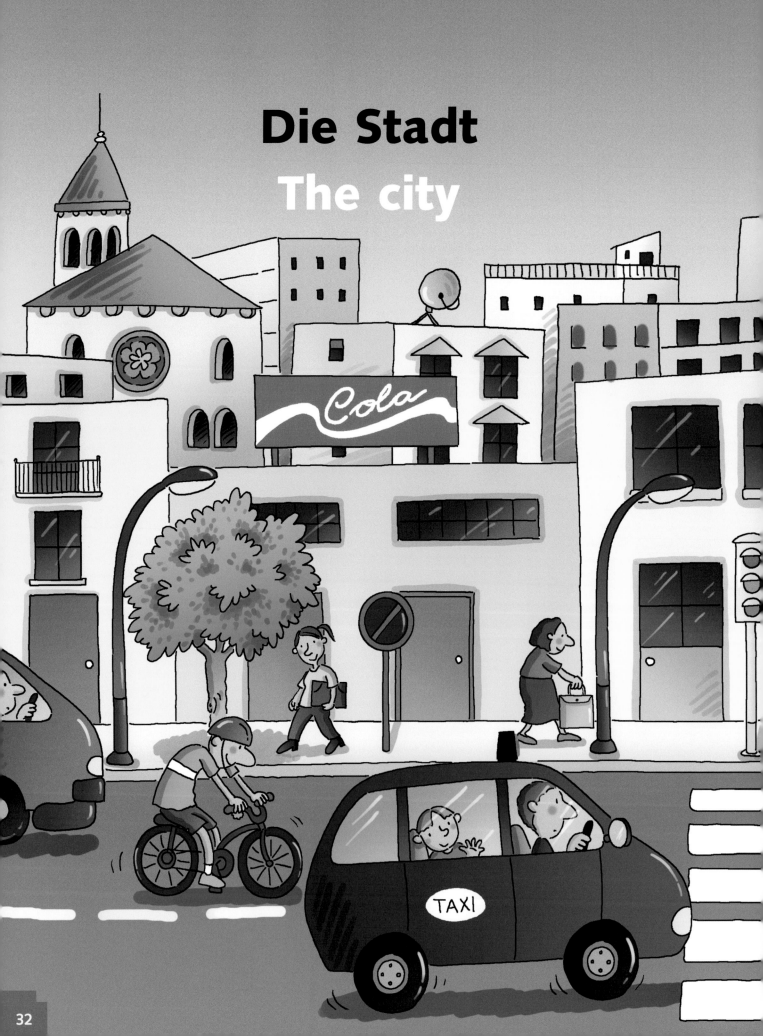

Finde diese Formen in dem Bild:
Find these shapes in the picture:

KREIS
CIRCLE

QUADRAT
SQUARE

DREIECK
TRIANGLE

RECHTECK
RECTANGLE

Welche Form hat ein/eine...?
What is the shape of a...?

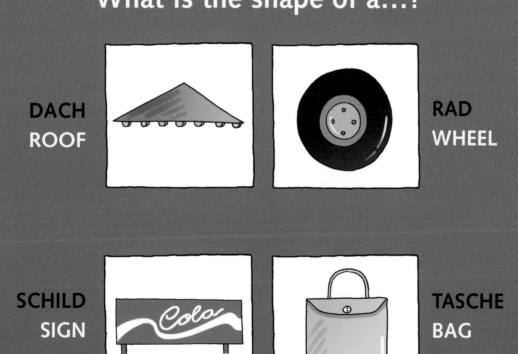

DACH
ROOF

RAD
WHEEL

SCHILD
SIGN

TASCHE
BAG

Unsere Strasse
Our street

GEBÄUDE
BUILDING

BAND
BANK

ZEBRASTREIFEN
ZEBRA CROSSING

BÜRGERSTEIG
PAVEMENT

STRASSE
ROAD

WOLKENKRATZER
SKYSCRAPER

BUSHALTESTELLE
BUS STOP

KAUFLADEN
SHOP

KIRCHE
CHURCH

GLOCKE
BELL

AMPEL
TRAFFIC LIGHTS

STRASSENLATERNE
STREET LAMP

MARKISE
AWNING

RESTAURANT
RESTAURANT

PARK
PARK

DENKMAL
MONUMENT

TELEFONZELLE
PHONE BOX

ABWASSERKANAL
SEWER

BRIEFKASTEN
POSTBOX

HOTEL
HOTEL

KRANKENHAUS
HOSPITAL

VERKEHRSSCHILD
TRAFFIC SIGN

UTOFAHRER
DRIVER

FUSSGÄNGER
PEDESTRIAN

RATHAUS
TOWN HALL

THEATER
THEATRE

BIBLIOTHEK
LIBRARY

KINO
CINEMA

Die Reise
The trip

AUTO
CAR

MOTORRAD
MOTORBIKE

FEUERWEHRAUTO
FIRE ENGINE

LENKRAD
STEERING
WHEEL

FAHRRAD
BICYCLE

STURZHELM
HELMET

LENKER
HANDLEBARS

SATTEL
SADDLE

PARKPLATZ
CAR PARK

KOFFER
SUITCASE

FLUGZEUG
AEROPLANE

ZUG
TRAIN

SCHIFF
SHIP

UNTERGRUNDBAHN
UNDERGROUND

KRANKENWAGEN
AMBULANCE

BUS
BUS

TAXI
TAXI

KRAN
CRANE

HUBSCHRAUBER
HELICOPTER

GARAGE
GARAGE

LIEFERWAGEN
VAN

SICHERHEITSGURT
SEAT BELT

PEDALE
PEDAL

WAGEN
CARRIAGE

FENSTER
WINDOW

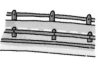

AUTOBAHN
HIGHWAY

ZUGFÜHRER
TRAIN DRIVER

LASTWAGEN
LORRY

Was würdest du gerne tun, wenn du
What would you like to do when you

ARCHITEKT
ARCHITECT

MÜLLMANN
REFUSE
COLLECTOR

HAUSMEISTER
CONCIERGE

BRIETRÄGERIN
POSTWOMAN

INFORMATIKER
IT SPECIALIST

DETEKTIV
DETECTIVE

APOTHEKER
PHARMACIST

FRISEUR
HAIRDRESSER

OBER
WAITER

LADENINHABER
SHOPKEEPER

chsen bist?

w up?

MALER
PAINTER

SCHRIFTSTELLER
WRITER

GÄRTNER
GARDENER

STRASSENKEHRER
STREET
SWEEPER

BALLERINA
DANCER

KOCH
COOK

POLIZIST
POLICEMAN

MECHANIKER
MECHANIC

FOTOGRAF
PHOTOGRAPHER

KRANKENSCHWESTER
NURSE

DOKTOR
DOCTOR

VERKÄUFER
SALESMAN

SCHAUSPIELERIN
ACTRESS

JOURNALIST
JOURNALIST

MUSIKER
MUSICIAN

WISSENSCHAFTLER
SCIENTIST

SÄNGERIN
SINGER

TAXIFAHRER
TAXI DRIVER

Sport
Sports

HOCHSPRUNG
HIGH JUMP

WEITSPRUNG
LONG JUMP

HÜRDEN
HURDLES

GYMNASTIK BAND
GYMNASTICS RIBBON

SCHLITT-SCHUHLAUFEN
ICE SKATING

ROLL-SCHUHLAUFEN
ROLLER SKATING

KORB
BASKET

BADEMÜTZE
SWIMMING CAP

BASKETBALL
BASKETBALL

BADESCHUHE
FLIP-FLOPS

TRAININGSANZUG
TRACKSUIT

MATRAZE
MAT

FUSSBALL
FOOTBALL

GYMNASTIK
GYMNASTICS

PURZELBAUM
SOMERSAULT

HANDSTAND
HANDSTAND

KNIESCHÜTZER
KNEE PADS

TENNIS
TENNIS

ROLLSCHUH
ROLLER
SKATE

STRANDVOLLEYBALL
BEACH
VOLLEYBALL

PING-PONG
PING-PONG

BADEANZUG
SWIMSUIT

JUDO
JUDO

SPIELER
PLAYER

TURNANZUG
LEOTARD

SCHWIMMEN
SWIMMING

NETZ
NET

TENNISSCHLÄGER
RACKET

Die Stadt
The city

AUF DEN BUS WARTEN
TO WAIT FOR THE BUS

ANRUFEN
TO MAKE A PHONE CALL

ÜBERQUEREN
TO CROSS

AUTOFAHREN
TO DRIVE

PARKEN
TO PARK

MIT DEM SCHIFF FAHREN
TO SAIL

MIT DEM ZUG FAHREN
TO GO BY TRAIN

MIT DEM FAHRRAD FAHREN
TO RIDE A BICYCLE

ZEIGEN
TO POINT

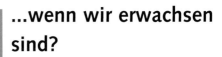

... wenn wir reisen?

...when we travel?

...wenn wir Sport treiben?

...when we play sports?

...wenn wir erwachsen sind?

...when we are adults?

PUNKTE ERZIELEN
TO SCORE

SICH AUSRUHEN
TO REST

SCHWITZEN
TO SWEAT

SCHIESSEN
TO SHOOT

IN DIE PFEIFFE BLASEN
TO BLOW A WHISTLE

ARBEITEN
TO WORK

HEILEN
TO CURE

UNTERSUCHEN
TO INVESTIGATE

KOCHEN
TO COOK

Tiere und Pflanzen
Animals and plants

EINS
ONE

ZWEI
TWO

DREI
THREE

VIER
FOUR

FÜNF
FIVE

SECHS
SIX

SIEBEN
SEVEN

ACHT
EIGHT

NEUN
NINE

ZEHN
TEN

Wie viele sind es?
How many are there?

EICHHÖRNCHEN
SQUIRREL

MAUS
MOUSE

EIDECHSE
LIZARD

SCHMETTERLING
BUTTERFLY

MARIENKÄFER
LADYBIRD

KIEFER
PINE

ROSE
ROSE

TULPE
TULIP

MARGHERITE
DAISY

FLIEDER
LILAC

Lasst uns auf den Bauernhof gehen
Let's go to the farm

HUHN
HEN

PFERD
HORSE

ZIEGE
GOAT

HAHN
COCK

TRAKTOR
TRACTOR

WASSERKANNE
WATERING CAN

HARKE
HOE

SCHUBKARRE
WHEELBARROW

BAUER
FARMER

TEICH
POND

KÜCKEN
CHICK

ENTE
DUCK

SCHWEIN
PIG

ESEL
DONKEY

KANINCHEN
RABBIT

SCHAF
SHEEP

KUH
COW

FROSCH
FROG

TRUTHAHN
TURKEY

KATZE
CAT

LAMM
LAMB

GEFURCHTES FELD
PLOUGHED FIELD

HEUBODEN
HAYLOFT

GEMÜSEGARTEN
VEGETABLE GARDEN

GANS
GOOSE

SCHWEINESTALL
PIGSTY

HOF
FARMYARD

STALL
STABLE

Lasst uns in den Zoo gehen
Let's go to the zoo

LÖWE
LION

LEOPARD
LEOPARD

BRAUNBÄR
BROWN BEAR

EISBÄR
POLAR BEAR

PANTER
PANTHER

TIGER
TIGER

RENTIER
REINDEER

ELEFANT
ELEPHANT

NASHORN
RHINO

GORILLA
GORILLA

NILPFERD
HIPPO

ZEBRA
ZEBRA

GIRAFFE
GIRAFFE

PANDA
PANDA BEA

KOALABÄR
KOALA

AFFE
MONKEY

ADLER
EAGLE

GEIER
VULTURE

NEST
NEST

STORCH
STORK

EULE
OWL

PAPAGEI
PARROT

KÄNGURU
KANGAROO

PINGUIN
PENGUIN

KAMEL
CAMEL

SCHLANGE
SNAKE

TAUBE
PIGEON

SPATZ
SPARROW

Lasst uns das Aquarium besuchen
Let's go to the aquarium

HAI
SHARK

MURÄNE
MORAY

ROCHEN
RAYFISH

ANEMONENFISCH
CLOWNFISH

SCHILDKRÖTE
TORTOISE

SEESTERN
STARFISH

SEEIGEL
SEA URCHIN

TINTENFISCH
SQUID

KRAKEN
OCTOPUS

QUALLE
JELLYFISH

MUSCHEL
MUSSEL

SEEHECHT
HAKE

SEEZUNGE
SOLE

ALGE
SEA WEED

KRABBE
CRAB

SARDINE
SARDINE

HUMMER
LOBSTER

VENUSMUSCHEL
CLAM

KABELJAU
COD

SANDSCHNECKE
WINKLE

KRABBE
PRAWN

NAPFSCHNECKE
LIMPET

SEELÖWE
SEAL

KILLERWAL
KILLER WHALE

DELFIN
DOLPHIN

SEEHUND
SEAL

WAL
WHALE

WALROSS
WALRUS

Tiere und Pflanzen
Animals and plants

MANN
MAN

FRAU
WOMAN

HUND
DOG

FISCH
FISH

HINAUSLEHNEN
TO LEAN OUT

SÄEN
TO SOW

SCHWIMMEN
TO SWIM

HINEINGEHEN
TO GO IN

HINAUSGEHEN
TO GO OUT

Wer ist das?
Who is it?

Was für ein Tier ist es?
What animal is it?

Was machen sie?
What do they do?

ÖFFNEN
TO OPEN

SCHLIESSEN
TO CLOSE

FÜTTERN
TO FEED

FLIEGEN
TO FLY

GRÜSSEN
TO SAY HELLO

BELLEN
TO BARK

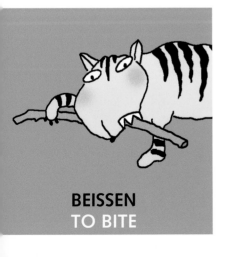

BEISSEN
TO BITE

KLETTERN
TO CLIMB

SPAZIERENGEHEN
TO TAKE A STROLL

DEUTSCH

ENGLISH

A B C D **E** F G **H** I J K **L** M N Ñ O P Q R S T U V W X Y Z

A

ABFALLEIMER 19
ABWASSERKANAL 35
ACHT 45
ADLER. 49
AFFE 49
ALGE. 50
AMPEL 34
ANEMONENFISCH 50
ANRUFEN 42
APOTHEKER 38
APPLAUDIEREN 11
AQUARIUM 27
ARBEITEN 43
ARCHITEKT. 38
ARM 20
AUF DEN BUS WARTEN . 42
AUFPRALLEN LASSEN. . . 30
AUGE 20
AUSSEN. 31
AUTO 36
AUTOBAHN 37
AUTOFAHREN 42
AUTOFAHRER. 35

B

BABY. 6
BAD. 21
BADEANZUG. 41
BADEMÜTZE. 40
BADESCHUHE. 40
BALKON 13
BALL 28
BALLERINA 39
BALLON 9
BALLPOOL 8
BAND 34
BANK 28
BARFUSS. 9
BASKETBALL 40
BAUER. 46
BAUM 28
BAUSTEINE 8
BEDDECKE 16
BEIN 20
BEISSEN. 53
BELEGTES BROT 28
BELLEN 53
BESEN 19
BETT 22
BIBLIOTHEK 35

BILD 14
BILDKARTEN 28
BINDEN. 11
BLÄTTER 29
BLASEN 11
BLATT PAPIER 26
BLAU. 25
BLEISTIFT 27
BLONDES HAAR 5
BLUMENTOPF. 29
BODEN 15
BRAUN 25
BRAUN BÄR 48
BRIEFKASTEN 35
BRIETRÄGERIN 38
BRILLE. 29
BROT 19
BRÖTCHEN. 8
BRÜDER 6
BRUST. 20
BUCH 14
BÜGELEISEN 22
BÜGELN 23
BÜRGERSTEIG. 34
BUS 37
BUSHALTESTELLE 34

C

CAFETIERE PERCOLATOR 19
COMPUTER 26
COMPUTERSPIEL 9
COUSIN 6
COUSINE 6

D

DACH 33
DECKE. 15
DECKE. 17
DELFIN 51
DENKMAL. 35
DETEKTIV 38
DICK 5
DOKTOR. 39
DREI 45
DREIECK 33
DREIRAD. 9
DUNKLES HAAR 5
DÜNN. 5
DUSCHE 22
DUSCHEN 23
DVD 14

E

EICHHÖRNCHEN 45
EIDECHSE 45
EIMER 29
EINS 45
EISBÄR 48
ELEFANT 48
ELLBOGEN 20
ENKEL 6
ENKELIN 6
ENTE 47
ESEL 47
ESSEN 23
EULE 49

F

FAHRRAD 36
FALLEN 11
FALTER 27
FARBEN. 27
FENSTER 13
FENSTER 37
FERNSEHER. 14
FEUERWEHRAUTO 36
FINGER 20
FISCH 18
FISCH 52
FLAGGE. 9
FLASCHE 15
FLEISCH 18
FLIEDER. 45
FLIEGEN 53
FLUGZEUG 37
FOTOGRAF. 39
FRAU. 52
FREUNDE 9
FRISEUR 38
FROSCH 47
FRÜCHTE 18
FRÜHSTÜCKSFLOCKEN . 19
FÜNF. 45
FUSS 20
FUSSBALL 40
FUSSGÄNGER 35
FÜTTERN. 53

G

GABEL. 15
GÄHNEN. 11
GANS 47
GARAGE 37

ARDINE 14
ÄRTNER 39
EBÄUDE 34
EFRIERTRUHE 19
EFURCHTES FELD 47
EIER 49
EIGE 7
ELANGWEILT 7
ELB 25
EMÜSE 19
EMÜSEGARTEN 47
ESCHIRR-
SPÜLMASCHINE 19
IRAFFE 48
LAS 14
LAS 22
LATTES HAAR 5
LOCKE 34
LÜCKLICH 7
LÜHBIRNE 7
ORILLA 48
RABSTICHEL 26
ROSS 5
ROSSMUTTER 6
ROSSVATER 6
RÜN 25
RÜSSEN 53
UITARRE 7
YMNASTIK 40
YMNASTIK BAND 40

AHN 46
AI 50
ALS 21
AMSTER 27
AND 20
ANDPUPPE 8
ANDSCHUHE 29
ANDSTAND 41
ANDTUCHHALTER 21
ARKE 46
AUSMEISTER 38
AUSSCHUHE 17
EILEN 43
ERAUSGEHEN 52
ERUNTERRUTSCHEN . . 30
EUBODEN 47
I-FI 15
INAUSGEHEN 52
INEINGEHEN 52
INTERN 20

HOCHSTEIGEN 30
HOCHSPRUNG 40
HOF 47
HOSE 17
HOTEL 35
HUBSCHRAUBER 37
HUHN 46
HUMMER 51
HUND 52
HÜPFSEIL 29
HÜRDEN 40

I

IN DIE PFEIFFE BLASEN . . 43
INFORMATIKER 38
INNEN 31

J

JACKE 16
JALOUSIE 13
JOGGINGSCHUHE 17
JOGURT 18
JOJO 28
JOURNALIST 39
JUDO 41

K

KABELJAU 51
KÄFIG 26
KAMEL 49
KAMM 22
KÄMMEN 23
KÄNGURU 49
KANINCHEN 47
KARTEN 8
KATZE 47
KAUFLADEN 34
KEGEL 8
KEKS 19
KERZEN 8
KIEFER 45
KILLERWAL 51
KINDERBETT 17
KINO 35
KIRCHE 34
KLAVIER 7
KLEBESTIFT 26
KLEID 17
KLEIDERBÜGEL 17
KLEINER VOGEL 29
KLETTERN 53
KLOPAPIER 21

KNET 27
KNIE 20
KNIEN 31
KNIESCHÜTZER 41
KNÖCHEL 20
KNOPF 17
KOALABÄR 49
KOCH 39
KOCHEN 43
KOFFER 36
KOMISCH 7
KONFETTI 7
KOPFKISSEN 17
KORB 40
KRABBE 51
KRAKEN 50
KRAN 37
KRANKENHAUS 35
KRANKENSCHWESTER . . 39
KRANKENWAGEN 37
KREIDE 26
KREIS 33
KREISEL 28
KRUG 15
KÜCHE 18
KUCHEN 9
KÜCHENSPÜLE 19
KÜCKEN 47
KUH 47
KÜHLSCHRANK 18
KURZES HAAR 5
KÜSSEN 10

L

LACHEN 30
LADENINHABER 38
LAMM 47
LAMPE 14
LANGES HAAR 5
LAPPEN 22
LASTWAGEN 37
LÄTZCHEN 26
LAUTSPRECHER 15
LEHRER 30
LEINTUCH 17
LENKER 36
LENKRAD 36
LEOPARD 48
LESEN 10
LIEFERWAGEN 37
LILA 25
LIMONADE 9

A
B
C
D
E
F
G
H
I
J
K
L
M
N
Ñ
O
P
Q
R
S
T
U
V
W
X
Y
Z

A
B
C
D
E
F
G
H
I
J
K
L
M
N
Ñ
O
P
Q
R
S
T
U
V
W
X
Y
Z

LINEAL 27
LOCKIGES HAAR 5
LÖFFEL 22
LÖWE 48
LUDO 8

M
MALER 39
MANN. 52
MÄPPCHEN 26
MARGHERITE 45
MARIENKÄFER 45
MARKISE. 34
MATRAZE 40
MAUS 45
MECHANIKER. 39
MESSER. 15
MIKROWELLE 19
MILCH 19
MIT DEM FAHRRAD
   FAHREN 42
MIT DEM SCHIFF
   FAHREN 42
MIT DEM ZUG FAHREN . 42
MORGENMANTEL 16
MOTORRAD. 36
MÜDE. 7
MÜLLMANN. 38
MUND 21
MURÄNE. 50
MURMELN 28
MUSCHEL 50
MUSIKER. 39
MUTTER 6

N
NACHBAR. 13
NACHTHEMD 16
NAPFSCHNECKE. 51
NASE. 21
NASHORN 48
NEFFE 10
NEST 49
NETZ 41
NEUN 45
NICHTE 10
NILPFERD 48
NOTIZBUCH 27

O
OBEN 31
OBER. 38

OFEN 19
ÖFFNEN 53
OHR 21
ONKEL 10
ORANGE 25

P
PANDA 48
PANTER. 48
PAPAGEI 49
PAPIERFLUGZEUG. 29
PARK 35
PARKEN. 42
PARKPLATZ. 36
PEDALE 37
PFANNE 18
PFEIFFE 28
PFERD 46
PINGUIN 49
PING-PONG 41
PINSEL. 27
PIRATENSCHIFF 9
POLIZIST. 39
PULLOVER 16
PUNKTE ERZIELEN 43
PUPPEN. 9
PURZELBAUM. 41
PUTZEN. 23
PUZZLE 8

Q
QUADRAT. 33
QUALLE 50

R
RAD 33
RADIERGUMMI 26
RATHAUS 35
RECHEN 29
RECHTECK 33
REDEN. 10
REGAL. 14
REGAL. 27
REIFEN 29
REISSVERSCHLUSS 17
RENNEN 31
RENTIER 48
RESTAURANT 34
ROBOTER 9
ROCHEN. 50
ROCK 16

ROHR 13
ROLLSCHUH. 41
ROLLSCHUHLAUFEN . . . 40
ROSE. 45
ROT 25
RUCKSACK 29
RÜCKEN 20
RUTSCHE 28

S
SÄEN. 52
SAFT 19
SALZFÄSSCHEN 15
SAND 29
SANDSCHNECKE. 51
SÄNGERIN. 39
SARDINE. 51
SATTEL 36
SAUBER. 9
SCHAF. 47
SCHAUFEL 29
SCHAUKELN 28
SCHAUSPIELERIN 39
SCHIEDSRICHTER 30
SCHIESSEN 43
SCHIFF 37
SCHILD 33
SCHILDKRÖTE 50
SCHLAFANZUG. 16
SCHLAFEN 23
SCHLANGE 49
SCHLEIFE. 29
SCHLIESSEN 53
SCHLITTSCHUHLAUFEN. 40
SCHLOSS 9
SCHLÜPFER. 16
SCHMETTERLING 45
SCHMUTZIG. 9
SCHOKOLADE 19
SCHORNSTEIN 13
SCHRANK 17
SCHREIBTISCH 17
SCHREIEN 10
SCHRIFTSTELLER. 39
SCHUBKARRE 46
SCHUBLADE 16
SCHUHE 17
SCHUHE TRAGEND 9
SCHULTER. 20
SCHWAMM 21
SCHWARZ. 25

CHWEIN 47
CHWEINESTALL 47
CHWESTER 6
CHWIMMEN 41
CHWIMMEN 52
CHWITZEN 43
CIENTIST 39
CISSORS 27
COOTER 8
ECHS 45
EEHECHT 50
EEHUND 51
EEIGEL 50
EELÖWE 51
EESTERN 50
EEZUNGE 50
EIFE 21
ERVIETTE 14
ESSEL 14
ICH ANSCHAUEN 23
ICH AUSRUHEN 43
ICHERHEITSGURT 37
IEB 18
IEBEN 45
INGEN 11
ITZEN 31
KATEBOARD 9
CHAF 47
OCKEN 17
OFA 14
OHN 6
PATZ 49
PAZIERENGEHEN 53
PIEGEL 22
PIELER 41
PIELKÜCHE 9
PITZER 27
PRINGEN 30
TALL 47
TECKER 15
TEHEN 31
TIEFEL 17
TIFT 27
TIRN 20
TRAND VOLLEY BALL . . 41
TRASSE 34
TRASSENLATERNE 34
TRASSENKEHRER 39
TREICHELN 11
TOCKBETTEN 16
TORCH 49
TUFEN 13

STUHL 27
STURZHELM 36

T
TABLETT 18
TAFEL 27
TAMBURIN 7
TANTE 10
TANZEN 11
TASCHE 33
TAUBE 49
TAXI 37
TAXIFAHRER 39
TEICH 46
TELEFON 15
TELEFONZELLE 35
TELLER 15
TENNIS 41
TENNISSCHLÄGER 41
TEPPICH 15
TOILETTE 21
TOPF 19
TOR 28
TORWART 30
TRAININGSANZUG 40
TRAKTOR 46
TRAURIG 7
TRINKEN 23
TROMPETE 7
TRUTHAHN 47
T-SHIRT 17
TIGER 48
TINTENFISCH 50
TISCH 27
TISCHDECKE 14
THEATER 35
TOCHTER 6
TRINKBRUNNEN 28
TROMMEL 7
TULPE 45
TÜR 13
TURNANZUG 41

U
ÜBERQUEREN 42
UHR 15
UMARMEN 10
UNTEN 31
UNTERGRUNDBAHN . . . 37
UNTERHOSEN 17
UNTERSUCHEN 43

V
VASE 14
VATER 6
VENUSMUSCHEL 51
VERKÄUFER 39
VERKEHRSSCHILD 35
VERKLEIDUNG 9
VIER 45
VORHANG 14

W
WACHSSTIFTE 27
WAGEN 37
WAL 51
WALROSS 51
WANDGEMÄLDE 27
WASCHBECKEN 21
WASCHMACHINE 19
WASSER 28
WASSERHAHN 19
WASSERKANNE 46
WEINEN 30
WEISS 25
WEITSPRUNG 40
WERFEN 31
WISCHER 26
WOLKENKRATZER 34

X
XYLOPHON 7

Z
ZÄHNE 21
ZÄHNE PUTZEN 23
ZAHNBÜRSTE 22
ZAHNPASTA 21
ZAUN 13
ZEBRA 48
ZEBRASTREIFEN 34
ZEHN 45
ZEIGEN 42
ZIEGE 46
ZUCKERDOSE 18
ZUG 37
ZUGFÜHRER 37
ZUHÖREN 11
ZUNGE 21
ZWILLINGE 6
ZWEI 45

A
B
C
D
E
F
G
H
I
J
K
L
M
N
Ñ
O
P
Q
R
S
T
U
V
W
X
Y
Z

A B C D E F G H I J K L M N Ñ O P Q R S T U V W X Y Z

A

ACTRESS 39
AEROPLANE 37
AMBULANCE 37
ANKLE 20
ARCHITECT 38
ARM 20
ARMCHAIR 14
AUNT 10
AWNING 34

B

BABY 6
BACK 20
BACKPACK 29
BAG 33
BALCONY 13
BALL 28
BALL POOL 8
BALLOON 9
BANK 34
BAREFOOT 9
BASKETBALL 40
BASKETBALL NET 40
BATH 21
BEACH VOLLEYBALL . . . 41
BED 22
BELL 34
BENCH 28
BIB 26
BICYCLE 36
BISCUIT 19
BLACK 25
BLACKBOARD 27
BLANKET 17
BLIND 13
BLOND HAIR 5
BLUE 25
BOOK 14
BOOKSHELF 14
BOOTS 17
BORED 7
BOTTLE 15
BOTTOM 20
BOW 29
BREAD 19
BREAST 20
BROTHERS 6
BROWN 25
BROWN BEAR 48
BRUSH 19
BUCKET 29

BUILDING 34
BUILDING BLOCKS 8
BULB 7
BUNK BEDS 16
BUNS 8
BURIN 26
BUS 37
BUS STOP 34
BUTTERFLY 45
BUTTON 17

C

CAGE 26
CAKE 9
CAMEL 49
CANDLES 8
CAR 36
CARDS 8
CAR PARK 36
CARRIAGE 37
CASTLE 9
CAT 47
CEILING 15
CEREAL 19
CHAIR 27
CHALK 26
CHICK 47
CHIMNEY 13
CHOCOLATE 19
CHURCH 34
CINEMA 35
CIRCLE 33
CLAM 51
CLEAN 9
CLOCK 15
CLOTH 22
CLOWNFISH 50
COCK 46
COD 51
COFFEE POT 19
COLANDER 18
COMB 22
COMPUTER 26
COMPUTER GAME 9
CONCIERGE 38
CONFETTI 7
COOK 39
COT 17
COUSIN (2) 6
COW 47
CRAB 51
CRANE 37

CURLY HAIR 5
CURTAIN 14

D

DAISY 45
DANCER 39
DARK HAIR 5
DAUGHTER 6
DESK 17
DETECTIVE 38
DIRTY 9
DISHWASHER 19
DOCTOR 39
DOG 52
DOLLS 9
DOLPHIN 51
DONKEY 47
DOOR 13
DOWN 31
DRAWER 16
DRESS 17
DRESSING GOWN 16
DRIVER 35
DRUM 7
DUCK 47
DUSTER 26
DVD 14

E

EAGLE 49
EAR 21
EIDERDOWN 16
EIGHT 45
ELBOW 20
ELEPHANT 48
ERASER 26
EYE 20

F

FANCY DRESS 9
FARMER 46
FARMYARD 47
FATHER 6
FENCE 13
FINGER 20
FIRE ENGINE 36
FISH 18
FISH 52
FISHTANK 27
FIVE 45
FLAG 9
FLIP-FLOPS 40

LOOR 15
LOWERPOT 29
OLDER 27
OOT 20
OOTBALL 40
OREHEAD 20
ORK 15
OUNTAIN 28
OUR 45
REEZER 19
RIDGE 18
RIENDS 9
ROG 47
RUIT 18
RYING PAN 18
UNNY 7

ARAGE 37
ARDENER 39
IRAFFE 48
LASS 14
LASS 22
LASSES 29
LOVES 29
LUE STICK 26
OALKEEPER 30
OALPOST 28
OAT 46
OOSE 47
ORILLA 48
RANDAUGHTER 6
RANDFATHER 6
RANDMOTHER 6
RANDSON 6
REEN 25
UITAR 7
YMNASTICS 40
YMNASTICS RIBBON . . 40

AIRDRESSER 38
AKE 50
AMSTER 27
AND 20
ANDLEBARS 36
ANDSTAND 41
ANGER 17
APPY 7
AYLOFT 47
ELICOPTER 37
ELMET 36

HEN 46
HI-FI 15
HIGH JUMP 40
HIGHWAY 37
HIPPO 48
HOE 46
HOOPS 29
HORSE 46
HOSPITAL 35
HOTEL 35
HURDLES 40

I
ICE SKATING 40
INSIDE 31
IRON 22
IT SPECIALIST 38

J
JACKET 16
JELLYFISH 50
JIGSAW PUZZLE 8
JOURNALIST 39
JUDO 41
JUG 15
JUICE 19
JUMPER 16

K
KANGAROO 49
KILLER WHALE 51
KITCHEN 18
KNEE 20
KNEE PADS 41
KNICKERS 16
KNIFE 15
KOALA 49

L
LADYBIRD 45
LAMB 47
LAMP 14
LEAVES 29
LEG 20
LEOPARD 48
LEOTARD 41
LIBRARY 35
LILAC 45
LIMPET 51
LION 48
LITTLE BIRD 29
LIZARD 45

LOBSTER 51
LONG HAIR 5
LONG JUMP 40
LORRY 37
LUDO 8

M
MAN 52
MARBLES 28
MAT 40
MEAT 18
MECHANIC 39
MICROWAVE 19
MILK 19
MIRROR 22
MODELLING PASTE . . . 27
MONKEY 49
MONUMENT 35
MORAY 50
MOTHER 6
MOTORBIKE 36
MOUSE 45
MOUTH 21
MURAL 27
MUSICIAN 39
MUSSEL 50

N
NAPKIN 14
NECK 21
NEIGHBOUR 13
NEPHEW 10
NEST 49
NET 41
NET CURTAIN 14
NIECE 10
NIGHTDRESS 16
NINE 45
NOSE 21
NOTEBOOK 27
NURSE 39

O
OCTOPUS 50
ON YOUR KNEES 31
ONE 45
ORANGE 25
OUTSIDE 31
OVEN 19
OWL 49

A
B

C

D
E

F
G
H

I
J
K
L

M
N

Ñ
O
P

Q
R
S

T
U
V

W
X
Y

Z

A
B
C
D
E
F
G
H
I
J
K
L
M
N
Ñ
O
P
Q
R
S
T
U
V
W
X
Y
Z

P

PAINTBRUSH. 27
PAINTER 39
PAINTS 27
PANDA BEAR 48
PANTHER 48
PAPER PLANE 29
PARK. 35
PARROT 49
PAVEMENT 34
PEDAL. 37
PEDESTRIAN 35
PEN 27
PENCIL 27
PENCIL CASE 26
PENCIL SHARPENER 27
PENGUIN 49
PHARMACIST 38
PHONE BOX 35
PHOTOGRAPHER 39
PIANO. 7
PICTURE 14
PICTURE CARDS 28
PIG 47
PIGEON. 49
PIGSTY 47
PILLOW 17
PINE 45
PING-PONG 41
PIPE. 13
PIRATE SHIP 9
PLATE 15
PLAYER 41
PLOUGHED FIELD 47
PLUG. 15
POLAR BEAR. 48
POLICEMAN 39
POND 46
POSTBOX 35
POSTWOMAN 38
POT. 19
PRAWN. 51
PUPPET 8
PURPLE 25
PYJAMAS 16

R

RABBIT 47
RACKET. 41
RAKE. 29
RAYFISH 50
RECTANGLE 33

RED. 25
REFEREE 30
REFUSE COLLECTOR . . . 38
REINDEER 48
RESTAURANT 34
RHINO 48
ROAD 34
ROBOT 9
ROLLER SKATE 41
ROLLER SKATING 40
ROOF 33
ROSE. 45
RUBBISH BIN. 19
RUG 15
RULER. 27

S

SAD. 7
SADDLE. 36
SALESMAN 39
SALTCELLAR 15
SAND 29
SANDWICH. 28
SARDINE 51
SCIENTIST 39
SCISSORS 27
SCOOTER 8
SEA URCHIN 50
SEA WEED. 50
SEAL (2) 51
SEAT BELT 37
SEVEN. 45
SEWER 35
SHARK 50
SHEEP 47
SHEET 17
SHEET OF PAPER 26
SHELF 27
SHIP 37
SHOES. 17
SHOP 34
SHOPKEEPER 38
SHORT 5
SHORT HAIR. 5
SHOULDER 20
SHOVEL 29
SHOWER. 22
SIGN 33
SINGER 39
SINK 19
SISTER. 6
SITTING. 31

SIX. 45
SKATEBOARD 9
SKIPPING ROPE 29
SKIRT 16
SKITTLES 8
SKYSCRAPER. 34
SLIDE. 28
SLIPPERS 17
SNAKE. 49
SOAP 21
SOCKS 17
SOFA. 14
SOFT DRINKS 9
SOLE. 50
SOMERSAULT 41
SON 6
SPARROW. 49
SPEAKER 15
SPINNING TOP 28
SPONGE 21
SPOON 22
SQUARE 33
SQUID. 50
SQUIRREL 45
STABLE 47
STANDING 31
STARFISH 50
STEERING WHEEL 36
STEPS 13
STORK 49
STOUT 5
STRAIGHT HAIR 5
STREET LAMP 34
STREET SWEEPER 39
SUGAR BOWL 18
SUITCASE 36
SWIMSUIT 41
SWIMMING 41
SWIMMING CAP 40
SWINGS 28

T

TABLE 27
TABLECLOTH 14
TALL 5
TAMBOURINE. 7
TAP 19
TAXI 37
TAXI DRIVER. 39
TEACHER 30
TEETH 21
TELEPHONE 15

62

ELEVISION 14
EN 45
ENNIS 41
HEATRE 35
HIN 5
HREE 45
IGER 48
IRED 7
O APPLAUD 11
O BARK 53
O BITE 53
O BLOW 11
O BLOW A WHISTLE . . 43
O BOUNCE 30
O BRUSH YOUR TEETH 23
O CARESS 11
O CLEAN 23
O CLIMB 53
O CLOSE 53
O COMB 23
O COOK 43
O CROSS 42
O CRY 30
O CURE 43
O DANCE 11
O DRINK 23
O DRIVE 42
O EAT 23
O FALL 11
O FEED 53
O FLY 53
O GO BY TRAIN 42
O GO DOWN 30
O GO IN 52
O GO OUT 52
O GO UP 30
O HUG 10
O INVESTIGATE 43
O IRON 23
O JUMP 30
O KISS 10
O LAUGH 30
O LEAN OUT 52
O LISTEN 11
O LOOK AT YOURSELF 23
O MAKE A PHONE CALL 42
O OPEN 53
O PARK 42
O POINT 42
O READ 10
O REST 43
O RIDE A BICYCLE 42

TO RUN 31
TO SAIL 42
TO SAY HELLO 53
TO SCORE 43
TO SHOOT 43
TO SHOUT 10
TO SING 11
TO SLEEP 23
TO SOW 52
TO SWEAT 43
TO SWIM 52
TO TAKE A SHOWER . . . 23
TO TAKE A STROLL 53
TO TALK 10
TO THROW 31
TO TIE 11
TO WAIT FOR THE BUS . 42
TO WORK 43
TO YAWN 11
TOILET 21
TOILET PAPER 21
TONGUE 21
TOOTHBRUSH 22
TOOTHPASTE 21
TORTOISE 50
TOWEL RACK 21
TOWN HALL 35
TOY KITCHEN 9
TRACKSUIT 40
TRACTOR 46
TRAFFIC LIGHTS 34
TRAFFIC SIGN 35
TRAIN 37
TRAIN DRIVER 37
TRAINERS 17
TRAY 18
TREE 28
TRIANGLE 33
TRICYCLE 9
TROUSERS 17
TRUMPET 7
T-SHIRT 17
TULIP 45
TURKEY 47
TWINS 6
TWO 45

U
UNCLE 10
UNDERGROUND 37
UNDERPANTS 17
UP 31

V
VAN 37
VASE 14
VEGETABLE GARDEN . . . 47
VEGETABLES 19
VIOLIN 7
VULTURE 49

W
WAITER 38
WALRUS 51
WARDROBE 17
WASHBASIN 21
WASHING MACHINE . . . 19
WATER 28
WATERING CAN 46
WAX CRAYONS 27
WEARING SHOES 9
WHALE 51
WHEEL 33
WHEELBARROW 46
WHISTLE 28
WHITE 25
WINDOW 13
WINDOW 37
WINKLE 51
WOMAN 52
WRITER 39

X
XYLOPHONE 7

Y
YELLOW 25
YOGURT 18
YO-YO 28

Z
ZEBRA 48
ZEBRA CROSSING 34
ZIP 17

A
B
C
D
E
F
G
H
I
J
K
L
M
N
Ñ
O
P
Q
R
S
T
U
V
W
X
Y
Z

First published in the UK in 2008 by Wayland

© Cromosoma, SA y Televisió de Catalunya, 2008
© Grupo Editorial Bruño, S.L., 2008

Wayland
338 Euston Road
London NW1 3BH

Wayland Australia
Level 17/207 Kent Street
Sydney NSW 2000

Illustrations: from the original drawings of Roser Capdevila
Text: Isabel Carril
Translation into English: John Liddy
Translation into German: Isabel Rollings

ISBN 978 0 7502 5695 7
ISBN Cromosoma: 978-84-92419-19-7

Wayland is a division of Hachette Children's Books,
an Hachette Livre UK company.